ENDURANCE

Shackleton's Incredible Antarctic Expedition

Anita Ganeri

WAYLAND

First published in paperback in 2016
by Wayland

Text copyright © Wayland 2016
Illustrations © Wayland 2016

Wayland
An imprint of
Hachette Children's Group
Part of Hodder & Stoughton
Carmelite House
50 Victoria Embankment
London EC4Y 0DZ

Editor: Victoria Brooker
Design: Basement 68
Picture researcher: Shelley Noronha

Picture credits: Alamy: 28 © NORMA JOSEPH;
Dulwich College: 25, 32; Getty Images: 6 Mansell/
The LIFE Picture Collection; 7m Popperfoto; 11
Topical Press Agency; Frank Hurley/Scott Polar
Research Institute, University of Cambridge 12, 13t,
13b, middle, 14, 15, 19t, 19b; 20 Hulton Archive;
Jo Stewart, Shackleton Epic: 43; Library of
Congress: 5 t ,17, 21t, 21b, 23t, 30t, 30b;
Mary Evans: Photoshot 8, 18; Rex: 4m, 34;
Royal Geographical Association (with IBG): 16,
22, 24, 27m, 35; Shutterstock: 5m Triff; 7b
Iaroslav Neliubov; 10r raciro; 15 b Yongyut Kumsri;
23b Steve Allen; 26 Oskari Porkka; 27b and 36
jo Crebbin; 33t Mary Ann McDonald; 33b
hecke61; 4 and 41 Big RoloImages/Shutterstock;
9 BrAt82; wikicommons http://en.wikipedia.org 9,
10l, 29, 38, 39, 40, 42; Topham Picturepoint:
31; Victor McLindon 44-45 map artwork.

A CIP catalogue record for this book is
available from the British Library.
Dewey number: 919.8'9'04-dc23

ISBN: 978 0 7502 9709 7
Ebook ISBN: 978 0 7502 9415 7

10 9 8 7 6 5 4 3 2 1

MIX
Paper from
responsible sources
FSC® C104740

Printed in Dubai

An Hachette UK company
www.hachette.co.uk

Contents

ANTARCTIC DREAMS

The vast frozen land of Antarctica lies at the southernmost end of the world. The coldest, windiest continent on Earth, it is ringed by the planet's stormiest seas. It is no wonder that, for centuries, people could only guess that any land might be there, and marked it on maps as 'Terra Australis Incognita', or 'unknown southern land'.

The first people to discover Antarctica were whale- and seal-hunters. An American sealer, John Davis, may have made the first known landing in 1821. Two years later, a ship, captained by British sealer, James Weddell, sailed into the sea that now carries his name.

Whalers in Antarctica in the mid-19th century.

Expeditions

At the end of the 19th century and beginning of the 20th, expeditions were launched from several different countries, including Belgium, Britain, Germany and Sweden. The aim of these expeditions was to learn more about the science and geography of Antarctica, but the race was also on to become the first to reach the South Pole, whatever the cost.

Shackleton

Key among the explorers willing to risk their lives on the ice was Ernest Shackleton. Born in Ireland on 15 February 1874, Shackleton was the son of a doctor. He did not want to follow in his father's footsteps but, instead, joined the merchant navy as an apprentice and went away to sea at the age of 16. By the time he was just 24 years old, he had qualified as a master mariner, able to command a British ship anywhere in the world.

Ernest Shackleton

Antarctica statistics

Area: 14,200,000 square kilometres

Average thickness of ice: 1.9 kilometres

Lowest recorded temperature: -89.2 °C

Population: None permanent

Highest point: Vinson Massif - 4,897 metres

Biggest ice shelf: Ross Ice Shelf - 965 kilometres

HEADING SOUTH

In March 1900, Shackleton was working on the Union-Castle Line, carrying troops from Britain to South Africa to fight in the Boer War. On board, he met army officer, Cedric Longstaff, whose father was backing the National Antarctic expedition, then being organised in London. The expedition was to be led by Captain Robert Scott.

Shackleton was keen to join the expedition. He later told reporters that he had always been 'strangely drawn to the mysterious south'. Luckily, Longstaff's father was impressed by Shackleton, and helped to secure him a place.

On 17 February 1901, Shackleton was appointed third officer on the expedition's ship *Discovery*. His duties were listed as '*In charge of seawater analysis. Ward-room caterer. In charge of holds, stores and provisions...He also arranges the entertainments.*'

The Discovery in Antarctica.

Discovery left London on 31 July 1901, arriving in Antarctica in January 1902. From the start, the expedition was badly organised. More time was spent choosing costumes for a fancy dress party than the expedition's skis and equipment. Many of the men had never even slept in a tent before, and could not ski, sledge or handle a dog team – essential requirements for travelling on ice.

In November, Scott chose Shackleton and scientist, Edward Wilson, to accompany him on the march south towards the South Pole. Although they reached further south than anyone before, the journey was not a great success. The dogs fell ill and had to be destroyed, and all three men suffered from frostbite, scurvy and snow blindness. On the return journey, Shackleton fell seriously ill, and was eventually sent back home to England by Scott.

South Polar Times

One of Shackleton's duties was to edit the expedition's newspaper 'The South Polar Times'. It included photographs, features, cartoons, song lyrics and weather reports, illustrated with beautiful landscape paintings, mostly by Edward Wilson, the expedition artist.

'Broken down in chest returning southern sledge journey suffering scurvy and overstrain don't worry nearly well coming home.'

ERNEST SHACKLETON, cable home to future wife, Emily

Shackleton, Scott and Wilson at the start of a sledging trip.

THE GREAT SOUTHERN JOURNEY

Back home, Shackleton spent time working as a journalist and was elected secretary of the Royal Scottish Geographical Society. But his mind was constantly being drawn back to Antarctica, and he began to make plans to return, this time at the head of his own expedition. The aim of the expedition was, finally, to conquer the South Pole.

On 1 January 1908, the expedition's ship, *Nimrod*, sailed from New Zealand on the last leg of her journey to Antarctica. Hampered by ice and bad weather, Shackleton eventually set up base camp at Cape Royds on Ross Island. In their hut on the ice, 'The Boss', as Shackleton was called by the men, prepared his team for the great push south.

The specially adapted car that Shackleton took with him worked on firm ground but couldn't move in snow.

The 'Great Southern Journey' began on 19 October 1908. Shackleton and three others set off with four ponies to reach the South Pole. It was exhausting going. Every few steps, the ponies and men (who were not wearing skis) sank into the snow. On some days, howling blizzards made it impossible to leave their tents. Even so, by 9 January 1909, they were just 180 kilometres from the Pole, closer than anyone else had ever come.

By this time, however, the four men were in a terrible state, and Shackleton was forced to turn back to save their lives. The return journey was a race against starvation. At one point, Shackleton gave his own biscuit ration to Frank Wild. They arrived at Hut Point just in time to catch the *Nimrod* before it left for New Zealand.

The four men who set out to try to reach the South Pole.

'All the money that was ever minted would not have bought that biscuit and the remembrance of the sacrifice will never leave me.'

FRANK WILD, second-in-command

'The only comment he made to me about not reaching the Pole was "a live donkey is better than a dead lion, isn't it?" and I said "Yes, darling, as far as I am concerned."'

EMILY SHACKLETON, Shackleton's wife

CROSSING A CONTINENT

Shackleton returned home to a hero's welcome and was knighted by the king. He wrote a book about the expedition and travelled all over Europe and the USA, giving lectures. The South Pole was finally reached by Norwegian, Roald Amundsen, in December 1911. If Shackleton had plans to head south again, he needed a new goal.

A poster for one of Shackleton's lectures.

A Norwegian stamp celebrating Roald Amundsen reaching the South Pole.

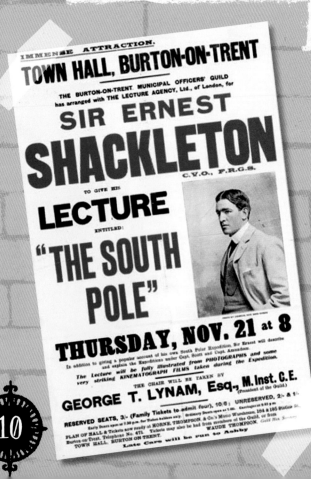

The journey that Shackleton decided to attempt was the 2,900-kilometre crossing of the continent from west to east, from the Weddell Sea, via the South Pole, to McMurdo Sound in the Ross Sea. It had never been done before. He began making plans for the expedition, randomly called the 'Imperial Trans-Antarctic Expedition'.

It was decided to take two ships. The *Endurance* would carry the main party into the Weddell Sea, aiming for Vahsel Bay. From there, a team of six, led by Shackleton, would begin the crossing. In the meantime, a second ship, the *Aurora*, would take a second group to McMurdo Sound, on the opposite side of the continent. This group would lay supplies of food and fuel as far as the Beardmore Glacier, for Shackleton's party to use.

The Endurance *sets sail from London on 1 August 1914.*

The *Endurance* was built in Norway by a famous firm of shipbuilders who specialised in designing ships for sealing and whaling at the Poles. To withstand the ice, she was built with a double-thickness wooden keel and an extra-thick bow. She was powered both by sail and by a coal-fired steam engine.

'From the sentimental point of view, it is the last great Polar journey that can be made. It will be a greater journey than the journey to the Pole and back... There now remains the largest and most striking of all journeys - the crossing of the Continent.'

ERNEST SHACKLETON

CHOOSING A CREW

It took Shackleton two years to raise enough money, through grants and gifts, to fund the expedition. He also promised to write a book about the trip, give lectures, and sold the rights to any films and photographs. All of these depended on one thing - that he survived!

Frank Wild

According to legend, Shackleton placed an advert for crew in a London newspaper. The advert read:

'Men wanted for hazardous journey. Low wages, bitter cold, long hours of complete darkness. Safe return doubtful. Honour and recognition in event of success.'

Frank Worsley

Mrs Chippy
(ship's cat)

It now seems that the advert may not have been real, but Shackleton had no problem finding volunteers for his trip. More than 5,000 people applied. From them, Shackleton selected his crew. He had an interesting way of choosing newcomers. If he liked the look of a man, he picked him. If he didn't, he didn't! As his second-in-command, he chose Frank Wild, who had been with him on the *Discovery* and *Nimrod* expeditions. New Zealander, Frank Worsley, was appointed captain of the *Endurance*. Worsley claimed that he applied for the job after learning about the expedition in a dream.

Endurance crew list

Ernest Shackleton – leader
William Bakewell – seaman
Percy Blackborow – stowaway, later steward
Alfred Cheetham – third officer
Robert Clark – biologist
Thomas Crean – second officer
Charles Green – cook
Lionel Greenstreet – first officer
Ernest Holness – fireman
Walter How – seaman
Hubert Hudson – second officer
Frank Hurley – photographer
Leonard Hussey – meteorologist
Reginald James – physicist

Alfred Kerr – second engineer
Timothy McCarthy – seaman
James McIlroy – surgeon
Thomas McLeod – seaman
Harry McNeish – carpenter
Alexander Macklin – surgeon
George Marston – artist
Thomas Orde-Lees – ski expert and storekeeper
Louis Rickinson – chief engineer
William Stephenson – stoker
John Vincent – boatswain
Frank Wild – second-in-command
James Wordie – geologist
Frank Worsley – captain

SETTING SAIL

By end of July 1914, everything was ready. The Endurance sailed from Plymouth on 8 August, heading for Argentina. Shackleton and Wild stayed behind to sort out some last-minute arrangements. They followed later, joining the ship in Buenos Aires.

The dogs being taken off the Endurance for training.

The *Endurance* took two months to cross the Atlantic Ocean and arrived in Buenos Aires on 9 October. The cook, who arrived on board drunk, was fired and Charles Green hired in his place. Frank Hurley, the expedition's official photographer, arrived from Australia. He had already travelled to Antarctica with Australian explorer, Douglas Mawson, and Shackleton greatly admired his work. Finally, 69 sledge dogs, shipped over from Canada, were brought on board and kennelled in stalls built on the main deck.

At 10.30 am on 26 October, the *Endurance* set sail for the remote island of South Georgia, off the southern tip of South America. It would be her last port of call. Shackleton was relieved to be on his way at last, but he also had the matter of a stowaway to deal with. Eighteen-year-old Percy Blackborow, had been smuggled on board by his friend, William Bakewell. He was found hiding in a locker and taken to see Shackleton. For a while, Shackleton raged at Blackboro, then he put his face close and said, 'Finally...if we run out of food, and anyone has to be eaten, you will be the first. Do you understand?'

Percy Blackborow

The *Endurance* reached Grytviken whaling station on South Georgia on 5 November 1914. The crew were met with depressing news. Ice conditions in the Weddell Sea were the worst for years.

Several of the Norwegian whaling captains suggested that Shackleton try again next season but Shackleton could not afford to wait. On 5 December 1914, the *Endurance* weighed anchor and set sail for Antarctica.

Grytviken whaling station as it is today.

'...now comes the actual work itself...the fight will be good.'

ERNEST SHACKLETON

INTO THE WEDDELL SEA

Shackleton ordered Worsley to set a course for the South Sandwich Islands. It was there, for the first time, that they encountered the thick pack ice that was to become their bitter enemy.

Finding a safe passage through the ice was painstakingly slow. Several times, the *Endurance* smashed into large ice floes. For two days, they sailed east, before finally turning south towards Vahsel Bay. At times, the ship could hardly push her way through the ice. Shackleton had hoped to cover around 310 kilometres a day. In fact, they were averaging less than 50 kilometres.

The Endurance *in full sail.*

In the New Year, the ice became looser and lighter and they were able to pick up speed. By 9 January, they had finally passed through the pack ice and could see the ocean stretching ahead. They continued to make excellent progress and, by 15 January, were only about 320 kilometres from Vahsel Bay.

It was too good to last. Over the next few days, heavy pack ice was sighted and they were heading straight towards it. Almost at once, they realised that this was a very different type of ice. It was thick, soft and mushy, and began to close in around the ship. On 24 January, a crack appeared in the ice in front of the ship. The sails were set and the engines put full speed ahead but the *Endurance* did not move. She was stuck fast. As Orde-Lees put it, 'frozen, like an almond in the middle of a chocolate bar'.

The Endurance *stuck in the pack ice.*

'I had been prepared for evil conditions in the Weddell Sea, but had hoped that the pack would be loose. What we were encountering was a fairly dense pack of a very obstinate character.'

ERNEST SHACKLETON

STUCK FAST

The men watched anxiously for signs that the pack was breaking up. But the days passed, and nothing changed. Efforts were made to cut a channel through the ice with saws, picks and chisels but it was a hopeless task. In late February, Shackleton had to admit defeat. There was no chance of freeing the ship - they would have to spend the winter on board.

Shackleton's dream of crossing the continent now lay in tatters but he tried hard to hide his disappointment from the crew. Instead, he set about making arrangements for the long winter.

The dogs were taken off the ship and kennelled in 'dogloos' on the ice. The officers and scientists were moved to a warmer part of the ship where sleeping cubicles were partitioned off and a long table and stove set up. They named their new quarters 'The Ritz', after the top London hotel.

The dogs by their 'dogloos' on the ice.

There was also the vitally important task of shooting seals for their meat and blubber (which was used for fuel). The dogs were divided into teams for training and for dragging seal carcasses back to the ship.

The main danger was boredom, especially as the days grew darker. The men spent their time giving each other haircuts, playing practical jokes, writing their diaries, listening to music, watching slide shows given by Hurley, and playing football on the ice. They also held dog races, although it was too dark to see to the end of the course.

Midwinter dinner on the Endurance *on 22 June 1915.*

Meanwhile, outside, the weather was getting worse with temperatures falling fast. All this time, the *Endurance* was stuck like a tiny speck in the ice, slowly being dragged in a circle by the wind and currents in the Weddell Sea.

The men playing football on the ice.

ABANDON SHIP

As spring approached, Shackleton hoped that the Endurance would be freed. In August, the ice around the ship began to break up but, instead of clearing a path for sailing, the ice was forced up under the ship, leaving her perched precariously on top.

For a few weeks, everything was quiet. Then, at the end of August, a series of huge shocks hit the ship. She groaned and creaked alarmingly as the ice battered her hull. The pressure continued to grow, squeezing the ship evermore tightly. On 24 October, the hull began to bend and splinter, and water began pouring in.

While the lifeboats and supplies were transferred to the ice, the men tried to pump the water out. It was a hopeless task. On 25 October, Shackleton gave the order to abandon ship.

Exhausted, the men set up camp on the ice. Next morning, they got ready to move on. The plan was to march to Paulet Island, around 560 kilometres away, where Shackleton knew that there were supplies of food. They would be dragging two of their three boats with them, loaded onto sledges. The journey began on 30 October, and quickly ran into trouble. The ice was a mass of hummocks and ridges, and it took three days to travel barely three kilometres.

Pulling the lifeboats across the ice.

Shackleton called the march off. He decided, instead, to make camp on a flat, solid-looking floe and hope for the drift of the ice to carry them closer to land. They called the camp 'Ocean Camp'. Over the following weeks, the men returned to the ship several times to collect supplies. The rest of the time was spent repairing the lifeboats, feeding the dogs and hunting for seals. In the evening, the team talked, played cards and listened to Hussey playing his banjo.

Shackleton and his men at Ocean Camp.

The Endurance *starting to sink.*

Then, on the afternoon of 21 November, they watched as the *Endurance* finally sank beneath the ice. 'I cannot write about it,' Shackleton noted that night in his diary.

PATIENCE CAMP

The loss of the Endurance was a terrible shock - now, it was just them and the ice. Time began to weigh heavily - there was little to do and still, the ice did not open. Shackleton decided that it was time to take action before the men got too downhearted.

Early on the morning of 23 December 1915, the men left camp and began to march across the ice. It was back-breaking work. As they struggled to pull the boats along, they sank up to their knees in the slushy snow.

Progress was painfully slow, not least because their boots constantly filled with water, making every step a nightmare. Finally, Shackleton had to admit defeat. The ice made it too risky to carry on.

The men set up camp, but with the ice melting at a dangerous rate, it was soon time to shift again. They nicknamed the new camp 'Patience Camp' - it was to be their home for the next three months. The days dragged by with little to do apart from sleep - difficult in soaking wet sleeping bags - and talk about food and the state of the wind.

Shackleton (right) with Frank Worsley who is skinning a penguin.

'The monotony of life here is getting on our nerves. Nothing to do, nowhere to walk, no change in surroundings, food or anything. God send us open water soon or we shall go barmy.'

LIONEL GREENSTREET, first officer

'...stewed penguin heart, liver, eyes, tongues, toes & God knows what else, with a cup of water...I don't think any of us will have nightmares from over-eating.'

HARRY McNEISH, carpenter

On 23 March 1916, Shackleton spotted a tiny black speck in the distance - land! It was one of the Danger Islets, which meant that, only 30 kilometres beyond it, lay Paulet Island, their destination. If the pack ice opened, they could reach it in a day. But the pack showed no signs of opening. In fact, they were soon drifting away from the land. Trapped on the ice, and with food running out, tempers began to fray.

Then, early one morning, the ice floe began to crack underneath their feet...

Penguins were an important source of food for the men.

ESCAPE FROM THE ICE

On 9 April, with a loud thump, the ice floe split right under the James Caird. The men dashed from their tents and dragged the boat to safety. Next morning, the ice cracked again, where Shackleton's tent had stood. Quietly, Shackleton gave the order, 'Launch the boats'.

Shackleton and his crew with the three lifeboats.

Quickly, the three boats - the *James Caird*, *Dudley Docker* and *Stancombe Wills* - were loaded with supplies and launched. The men began to row for their lives. They needed to reach open water and, already, the ice was closing in.

Built for hunting whales, the boats were sturdy enough but no match for the journey they now faced. That afternoon, they made good progress, then pitched camp on a floe for the night. But at 11 pm disaster struck. The ice cracked beneath one of the tents and Holness fell into the water in his sleeping bag. He was hauled out, freezing but alive.

Next day, they launched the boats again and, by mid-morning, found themselves in open ocean. It was the moment they had dreamed of, but quickly turned into a nightmare as the men were battered by icy winds and freezing spray. That night, they camped on another floe. During the night, the weather got worse. Ice lay all around them and their campsite was crumbling. If they stayed put, the ice could split at any moment. If they launched the boats, they would be smashed to pieces.

The James Caird on display at Dulwich College in London.

Suddenly, a channel cleared and the men rushed to the boats. The plan now was to head for King George Island, then on to Deception Island where there were food supplies. There was no more camping on ice floes. The men ate and spent the nights in the boats. Sleep was impossible - there was nowhere to lie down.

On 12 April, Worsley took a reading with his sextant to find their position. It was heart-breaking news. They were 35 kilometres further from land than when they had left Patience Camp three days before. Despite their best efforts, they had been going backwards.

LAND AT LAST

Once again, Shackleton was forced to change destination. They would head to Hope Bay about 200 kilometres away. By now, the men were in a pitiful state. Their clothes were frozen stiff and, for a third night running, there was no sleep. It was clear that they could not take much more.

Next morning, the destination changed again. The new plan was to take advantage of the wind and reach Elephant Island, now 160 kilometres away. Sails hoisted, they set off.

To boost their spirits, the men were given hot milk to drink and as much food as they could eat.

Just before midday, they sailed into the open ocean...straight into a huge, rolling swell that made the little boats pitch alarmingly. That night was worse than any that they had spent. It was so cold that the waves froze as they hit the boats. The men huddled in their sleeping bags, wiggling their toes to stop them from freezing. After a few hours, Blackborow lost all feeling in his feet.

Huge waves made life in the small boats very dangerous for all.

As the sun rose next morning, Elephant Island lay dead ahead, no more than 50 kilometres away. Shackleton was anxious to be off, but first they had to chip the ice from the boats - even the oars were frozen to the sides of the boats. By midday, they had covered half the distance. Exhausted and desperately thirsty, they needed one last push and they would be there.

Until now, the three boats had stayed together, with the *James Caird* towing the *Wills*. Now Shackleton ordered the *Docker* to try to land separately. Before long, she had disappeared into the dark. Shackleton, on the *James Caird*, feared the worst. As dawn broke, the *James Caird* and the *Wills* lay off the coast of Elephant Island with no sign of a landing place. Then, someone spotted a tiny, shingle beach, hidden behind a line of rocks. Reunited with the *Docker*, the boats headed for the shore.

Landing the lifeboats on Elephant Island.

ELEPHANT ISLAND

For the first time in 497 days, Shackleton and his men stood on solid land. But Elephant Island was a bleak place. Nobody lived there, and it was rarely visited by whalers or other ships. If they were to escape from the ice, they would need to go in search of help.

The men were deathly tired. They ate a meal of seal steaks, then unrolled their soaking sleeping bags and went to sleep. But the morning brought devastating news. It was too risky to stay on the beach - they would have to move again. Wild had found a sheltered spit of land, about 11 kilometres away, where there were plenty of penguins and seals for food, and ice from a glacier for melting into water. Early next morning, the men returned to the boats and headed to their new home at 'Point Wild'.

The rocky coast of Elephant Island.

Now, Shackleton turned his mind to escape. The only way to get help was for a small party to head to South Georgia - a perilous 1,300-kilometre crossing of some of the stormiest seas in the world. Shackleton selected five men to go with him - Worsley, as navigator, Crean, McNeish, Vincent and McCarthy. The chances of reaching South Georgia safely were small but they had no choice.

Using an old sledge, wooden packing cases and canvas sacks, McNeish rigged up a canvas cover for the boat. Then food, water and equipment were loaded on board. It included six reindeer sleeping bags, binoculars, a compass, a small medicine chest, cooking stoves, a few candles and some matches. At 12.30 pm on 24 April, 1916, the *James Caird* set sail.

Launching the James Caird *from Elephant Island.*

'Turned in and slept, as we had never slept before, absolute dead dreamless sleep, oblivious of wet sleeping bags, lulled by the croaking of the penguins.'

REGINALD JAMES, physicist

'We watched them until they were out of sight, which was not long, for such a tiny boat was soon lost to sight on the great heaving ocean...'

THOMAS ORDE-LEES, storekeeper

LEFT BEHIND

The men left behind on Elephant Island watched as the James Caird disappeared from sight. Now, there was nothing for them to do but wait. Frank Wild had been left in charge, with instructions to make for Deception Island the next spring if Shackleton had not returned.

The most urgent task was to build a decent shelter to protect them from the blizzards that swept the island. They had begun to dig a cave in the glacier but the ice was rock-hard and it was back-breaking work. Worse still, when they were inside the cave, the heat from their bodies caused the ice to melt.

Life on Elephant Island was very tough.

There was only one thing for it - the boats. Using stones from beach, they built the walls of a hut and placed the upturned boats on top as a roof. Then pieces of canvas and blankets were stretched all around to keep the wind out. Gradually, they made the hut more comfortable, sealing up the holes in the walls to keep the snow out and making blubber lamps. But it was still an utterly miserable place to be.

The two doctors - Macklin and McIlroy - were kept busy looking after their patients. Blackborow was the most seriously ill. The toes on his left foot were so badly frostbitten that gangrene had already set in. On 15 June, using the hut as a makeshift operating theatre and packing cases as a table, they decided to operate and amputate Blackborow's toes.

One by one, the days crept by as the men waited and watched out for a rescue ship. But, by the middle of August, two years since leaving London, they were beginning to lose hope.

'...living in a smoky, dirty, ramshackle little hut with only just sufficient room to cram us all in...- a horrible existence.'

ALEXANDER MACKLIN,
surgeon

'We are still enduring our existence here with patience, and time passes really fairly quickly in spite of the dreadful tedium. My mind is becoming terribly blank - I lie for hours without even so much as thinking in a sort of vacuous state.'

ALEXANDER MACKLIN,
surgeon

The men's living quarters on Elephant Island.

DESPERATE JOURNEY

Meanwhile, the men in the James Caird picked their way through the pack ice and out into the open ocean. There was no turning back now.

The men onboard settled into some sort of routine. At all times, three of them kept watch, while the others rested in the tiny, covered space in the bows. Ice settled thickly on the boat, threatening to sink her, and the men risked their lives to chip it away with an axe. Their woollen clothes were soaking wet, and sleeping and eating were almost impossible in the cramped conditions.

The James Caird *sailed across some of the stormiest seas on the planet.*

For days, the tiny boat was pounded and battered by huge seas and some of the biggest waves that Shackleton had ever seen. To make matters worse, their water supply was dangerously low. They needed to land, and quickly, but thick fog made it impossible to see if they were nearing land, or not.

Then, at last, on the morning of 8 May, they spotted seaweed and cormorants - sure signs of land. And there they were - the black cliffs of South Georgia just a few kilometres ahead. They had done it. Or had they? Huge waves and hurricane-force winds now made landing impossible, and risked wrecking the boat on the rocks. They had no choice but to sit it out.

On 10 May, the storm eased slightly and Shackleton decided to risk a landing. It was clear that some of the men would not survive another day at sea. It was time for one last, desperate effort. Spotting a tiny break in the reef, they rowed furiously for the shore.

Cormorants were a sign that land was near.

'Reindeer bags in such a hopeless sloppy slimy mess, smelling badly and weighing so heavily that we throw two of the worst overboard.'

FRANK WORSLEY, captain

'Things were bad for us in those days. The bright moments were those when we received our one mug of hot milk during the long, bitter watches of the night.'

ERNEST SHACKLETON

CROSSING THE LAND

At 5 pm, on 10 May 1916, the five men found themselves standing on the shores of South Georgia, the island they had sailed from 522 days before. They were close to exhaustion and desperately thirsty but they had achieved the impossible.

They had landed on the south side of the island, the opposite side to the whaling station at Stromness. Shackleton knew that the boat and some of the men would not survive a further long voyage. Instead, after a few days' rest, he sailed the *James Caird* to King Haakon Bay, about 11 kilometres away. From here, he, Worsley and Crean would try to cross the island by foot, a distance of only 45 kilometres, but over such hostile terrain that no one had ever attempted it before.

King Haakon Bay on South Georgia.

At around 3 am on 19 May, the three men set off, leaving their companions behind at 'Peggotty Camp'. They had no map to guide them, and no idea what lay ahead. What they found was fog so thick that they had to rope together, and glaciers with treacherous crevasses. Three times, they climbed up mountains only to find no way down on the other side. Each time, they were forced to retrace their steps.

An albatross soaring over the Southern Ocean.

Well after 4 pm, they struggled to the top of another slope. The ridge at the top was so sharp that Shackleton could sit astride it. The way down seemed impossibly steep but they had no choice. It was getting colder, and they had no tents or sleeping bags. They had to get down...and quickly. Shackleton suggested that they slide. It seemed a ridiculous and terrifying suggestion, but it worked. Sitting on mats made from coiled-up ropes, they slid down the slope and into a snowbank.

Shackleton and his men faced unknown and hostile terrain.

'We had...albatross for lunch with 1 pint of gravy which beats all the chicken soup I ever tasted. I have just been thinking what our companions [on Elephant Island] would say if they had food like this.'

HARRY MCNEISH,
carpenter

MY NAME IS SHACKLETON

At 6.30 am the next morning, Shackleton heard a whistle. At 7 am, it sounded again. It was coming from the whaling station at Stromness, calling the men to work. It was the first sound that they had heard from the outside world since December 1914.

But their ordeal was not over yet. Looking down from the final ridge, they could see the whaling station, with boats in the bay and the tiny figures of men moving about. But the only way down was to lower themselves, one by one, by rope through an icy waterfall.

Stromness whaling station today.

At 4 pm, the figures of three men walked into the whaling station at Stromness. They looked like scarecrows. Their hair hung down to their shoulders, and their beards were filthy and matted. Their faces were black, apart from around their eyes, and their clothes hung off them in rags. The station foreman was puzzled. They had not come from a ship in the dock but from the direction of the mountains.

One of the men stepped forward and asked to be taken to the station manager, Thoralf Sorlle. The foreman led them to Sorlle's house. 'Who are you?' said Sorlle, opening his door. He looked shocked. 'My name is Shackleton,' Shackleton said.

After a long bath, a shave, new clothes and a hearty meal, Worsley was taken by whaling boat to rescue the three men at Peggotty Camp. The boat reached them the following morning. At first, the three men did not recognise Worsley because he had clean clothes and no beard. They arrived in Stromness on 22 May. It had been one of the most remarkable feats of survival that there had ever been.

'[The adze and the log-book'] were all we brought, except our wet clothes, from the Antarctic, which a year and a half before we had entered with a well-found ship, full equipment and high hopes.'

ERNEST SHACKLETON

Modern climbers retracing Shackleton's steps.

RESCUE MISSIONS

Shackleton now set about organising the rescue of the men left behind on Elephant Island. He arranged for the use of a large, wooden whaling boat, the Southern Sky. At 9 am on 23 May 1916, the Southern Sky steamed out of the bay with Shackleton on board.

At first, they made good progress but less than a week later, thick sea ice forced the *Southern Sky* to turn back. Within ten days, Shackleton had found a new ship but, again, she could not break through the ice. A third attempt was also called off. It was now the beginning of August, more than three months since the *James Caird* had left.

Finally, on 30 August, the 22 men on Elephant Island watched in amazement as a ship headed towards the beach with Shackleton on board. They were quickly evacuated and taken to Valparaiso, in Chile, where cheering crowds welcomed them back.

Shackleton, on board the Yelcho, rescued the men from Elephant Island.

One final rescue remained - the men of the Ross Sea party. They had been stranded at Cape Evans in McMurdo Sound for two years after the *Aurora* had been torn from its moorings and blown out to sea. After drifting for months, the *Aurora* had finally reached New Zealand. In December 1916, Shackleton joined the ship and sailed to rescue them, bringing them back to a heroes' welcome. Despite many hardships and the death of three members of the party, they had carried out their duties of laying supplies across the ice.

The men of the Ross Sea party.

'I stayed on deck to watch Elephant Island recede in the distance...I could still see my [jacket] flapping in the breeze on the hillside. No doubt it will flap there to the wonderment of gulls and penguins till one of our familiar [gales] blows it all to ribbons.'

ALEXANDER MACKLIN, surgeon

The Aurora.

LATER LIFE

When Shackleton returned to England in May 1917, Europe was in the middle of World War I. Shackleton was desperate to join the army but was too old and suffering from ill health. He worked briefly as a diplomat in Argentina before coming home in April 1918.

Back home, Shackleton spent his time giving lectures and writing his own account of the *Endurance* expedition, called *South*. Published in November 1919, it became a bestseller. But Shackleton was also dreaming of one last expedition to Antarctica.

The expedition left England on 17 September 1921, on board the *Quest*, a Norwegian sealing ship. The aim of the expedition was to sail around the continent. Shackleton was joined by many members of the *Endurance*'s crew, including Wild, Worsley, Macklin and McIlroy, keen to leave everything behind and travel with 'The Boss' again

The Quest *sailing underneath Tower Bridge in London.*

On 17 December, the day before the ship left Rio de Janeiro, Shackleton had a heart attack. Despite this, he insisted on continuing to South Georgia, which they reached on 4 January 1922. After visiting the whaling station, Shackleton seemed to be feeling better. He returned to the ship to write his diary, promising that they would have a late Christmas celebration the next day.

Early the next morning, Macklin was called to Shackleton's cabin. Shortly afterwards, Shackleton suffered another heart attack and died. He was buried in the Norwegian cemetery at Grytviken, with a rough cross marking his grave.

Shackleton's grave on South Georgia.

'The old smell of dead whale permeates everything. It is a strange and curious place... A wonderful evening. In the darkening twilight, I saw a lone star hover, gem like above the bay.'

ERNEST SHACKLETON

'I think this is as the Boss would have had it himself, standing lonely on an island far from civilisation, surrounded by stormy tempestuous seas, and in the vicinity of one of his greatest exploits.'

ALEXANDER MACKLIN, surgeon

IN SHACKLETON'S FOOTSTEPS

For many years after Shackleton's death, he was outshone by **Captain Scott** as the greatest polar hero of the time. More recently, though, Shackleton's bravery and leadership skills have been recognised as truly heroic and the story of the Endurance expedition has become one of the greatest survival stories.

Statue of Shackleton outside the Royal Geographical Society in London.

Various expeditions followed in Shackleton's footsteps. In 1957-1958, an expedition led by British explorer, Vivian Fuchs, and New Zealander, Edmund Hillary, finally achieved Shackleton's dream. The expedition became the first to cross Antarctica from the Weddell Sea to the Ross Sea, via the South Pole. Travelling in six vehicles, the team covered 3,473 kilometres in 99 days.

In January 2013, almost 100 years after Shackleton, a team of British and Australian explorers set out to recreate Shackleton's boat journey from Elephant Island to South Georgia, then his crossing of the island. Led by Tim Jarvis, they used the same gear and clothing as Shackleton had in 1916, and the same kind of wooden lifeboat, called the *Alexandra Shackleton*, after Shackleton's grand-daughter. All that they had to eat was a mix of lard, Bovril and walnuts.

Like Shackleton, the team faced icebergs, storms and frostbite, and during the crossing of South Georgia, Jarvis slipped down a crevasse. At one point, bad weather forced them to spend 24 hours stuck on the mountains. 'Following in Shackleton's footsteps heightened my level of respect for what he achieved,' Jarvis said. 'He was a true pioneer.'

'For scientific leadership, give me Scott; for swift and efficient travel, Amundsen; but when you are in a hopeless situation, when there seems no way out, get down on your knees and pray for Shackleton.'

RAYMOND PRIESTLEY, explorer

Tim Jarvis and his team recreating Shackleton's epic journey.

MAP OF THE JOURNEY

This map shows the route that Shackleton's expedition took, from its departure from South Georgia on 5 December 1914 to Shackleton's eventual, triumphant return to the island on 20 May 1916.

1. 5 December 1914 - Endurance leaves South Georgia
2. 18 January 1915 - Endurance is stuck fast in the ice
3. Endurance drifts with the ice
4. Crew lose sight of land
5. 25 October 1915 - Shackleton gives order to abandon ship
6. Ocean Camp
7. 21 November 1915 - Endurance sinks
8. January - April 1916 - Patience Camp
9. 9 April 1916 - boats launched for Elephant Island
10. 24 April 1916 - James Caird heads for South Georgia
11. 10 May 1916 - James Caird lands on South Georgia
12. 19-20 May 1916 - crossing of South Georgia

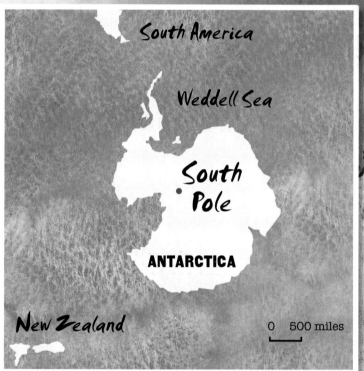

South America

Weddell Sea

South Pole

ANTARCTICA

New Zealand

0   500 miles

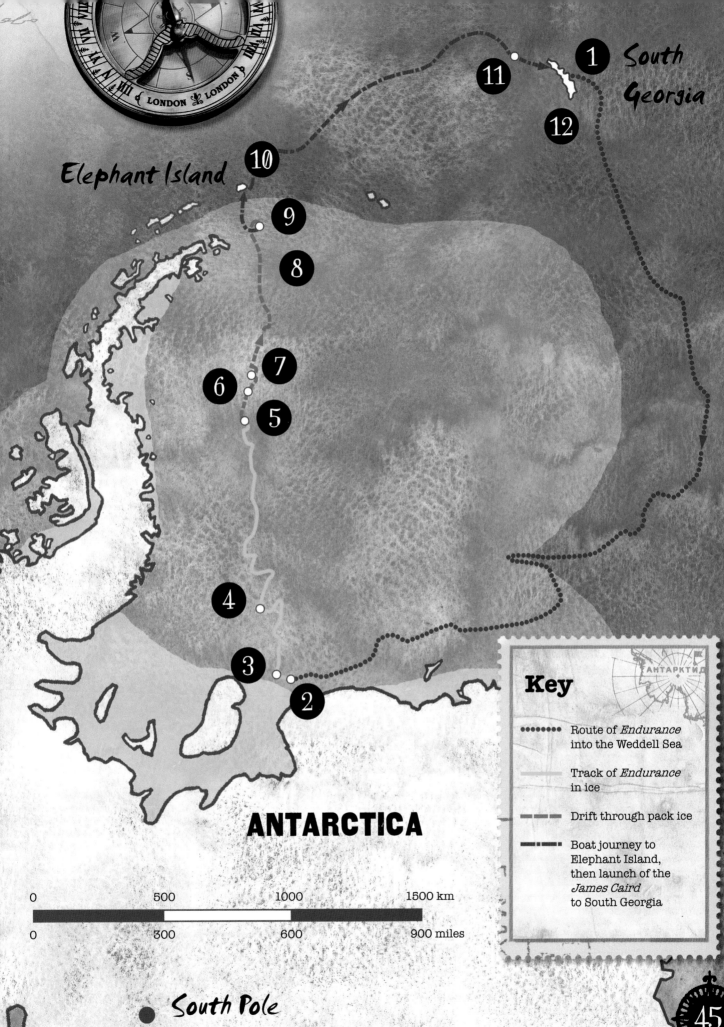

South Georgia

Elephant Island

ANTARCTICA

South Pole

Key

•••••• Route of *Endurance* into the Weddell Sea

━━━ Track of *Endurance* in ice

- - - Drift through pack ice

━·━·━ Boat journey to Elephant Island, then launch of the *James Caird* to South Georgia

0   500   1000   1500 km

0   300   600   900 miles

Glossary

amputate remove all or part of a limb

blubber thick layer of fat under an animal' skin boatswain

ship's officer who looks after a ship and its equipment

Bovril hot drink made from beef stock

bow front end of a ship

carcasses dead bodies of animals

crevasses deep cracks in a glacier

currents huge flows of water, like rivers, in the ocean

floe sheet of ice floating in the sea

frostbite damage to body parts when they get very cold

geologist scientist who studies rocks and the structure of the Earth

glacier slowly moving mass of ice

grants sums of money

keel structure running lengthways along the centre of the bottom of a ship

lard pig fat

master mariner professionally qualified sailor in charge of a ship

meteorologist scientist who studies the weather

navigator person in charge of finding the way

pack ice large stretch of floating ice, made from pieces that have clumped together

scurvy disease caused by lack of vitamin C

slide photograph mounted in small frame that can be shown on a screen

stoker person employed to look after a furnace (fire) and keep it burning

stowaway person who hides on board a ship, plane or other vehicle

terrain country, ground or landscape

ward-room officers' quarters (cabins) on a ship

DUN LAOGHAIRE, IRELAND - home to the Shackleton Endurance Exhibition which has on display more than 150 photographs taken by expedition photographer, Frank Hurley. There is also a full-size replica of the James Caird. The exhibition has toured the USA, Ireland, Spain and the UK. Shackleton, Tom Crean and Tim McCarthy were from Ireland.

DULWICH, LONDON - the James Caird, the lifeboat in which Shackleton made his epic journey, is on display at Dulwich College, Shackleton's old school. The boat can be viewed during school term time, although you need to make an appointment.

CAPE ROYDS, ANTARCTICA - the hut that Shackleton's crew built on the 1907-1909 Nimrod Expedition as the base for their attempt on the South Pole. It was fully restored between 2004-2008 to the condition in which Shackleton left it.

GRYTVIKEN, SOUTH GEORGIA - Shackleton's grave lies in the graveyard at Grytviken, alongside those of the whalers who died on the island. Today, a simple granite (stone) pillar marks the grave. It is inscribed with a quotation from Shackleton's favourite poet, Robert Browning. It reads 'I hold...that a man should strive to the uttermost for his life's set prize.' In 2011, Frank Wild's ashes were buried in a grave on the right-hand side.

SHACKLETON GAP, SOUTH GEORGIA - an ice-covered pass up to 300 metres high between King Haakon Bay and Possession Bay, South Georgia. It was part of the treacherous route taken by Shackleton in 1916.

Index